The Five

Be's

For Starting Out

Mickey Addison

Lead The Way Media
Kailua, Hawaii

The Five Be's for Starting Out

Cover bee image licensed through iStock.com

ISBN: 978-0-9960193-2-3

Published by: Lead The Way Media, Kailua, Hawaii

mickey@leadthewaymedia.com

This book is available through Lulu.com and via Mickey's website at mickeyaddison.com in paperback and ebook formats. Order forms are also in the back of the book.

DISCLAIMER
The views expressed in this book are those of the author and do not reflect the official policy or position of the United States Air Force, the Department of Defense or the U.S. Government.

For the Air Force Noncommissioned Officers Corps: today's heroes who daily turn young people into leaders and tomorrow's heroes.

Contents

Thank You

Thanks to all those who contributed, knowingly or unknowingly, to this book. To the many mentors who encouraged me to be the best man I could, thank you for your support. For all my bosses and teammates who endured my rants, my wild ideas, and my enthusiasm, thank you for your patience!

A special thanks to the noncommissioned officers who taught me so much about leadership and how to be an officer--many of you will never know the impact you had on me but it was and is significant.

Finally, thank you to my wife who has stood by me and encouraged me through my entire adult life. You are the reason I have the courage to face the day.

About this Book

This book is about how to live a full, successful, and happy life.

This is not a leadership book, yet good leaders practice these principles and espouse many of these ideas. It is not a religious book, although you are sure to see some common religious themes in some of the ideas presented. It is not a moralist's view, although you can certainly use the principles I describe to make good moral choices.

This book *is* a positive vision of who I would like to be, and who I want the ones around me to be. Do I always "walk the talk"? Of course not, few do. But I can say each time I haven't lived up to my own ideals, I have regretted it. *The Five Be*'s is a vision of a person who is able to face the world and live in it without being swept away by it. It's who I want to be.

Introduction

I stood in front of a group of sleepy young Airmen at the First Term Airmen's Center (FTAC) as they waited to hear what the old colonel had to say. With few exceptions, they were all approximately 19 years old and living away from home for the first time in their lives. They had all volunteered to serve their country in a time of war. Most of them were in kindergarten or elementary school during the 9/11 attacks.

> *"We are what we repeatedly do; excellence, then, is not an act but a habit."*
>
> *- Aristotle*

Before they appeared in their new Air Force blue uniforms in that FTAC classroom, they had successfully completed 12 weeks of Air Force Basic Military Training. In addition, they had attended Air Force Technical Training to learn the skills each would employ in their Air Force Specialty.

For their first six months in the Air Force, they had heard their leaders give them a lot of "don'ts." It was not just the Air

Force Military Training Instructors who had told them "don't"; they have been hearing that word a throughout their lives.

As we raise young people into adulthood, we put a great deal of effort into setting boundaries. In fact, most of what young people hear as they grow is a list of "don'ts." When we're very young, we hear "don't throw food on the floor", "don't speak disrespectfully to your elders", and "don't take toys away from your friends." As we grow, the "don'ts" begin to pile up: *don't* play in the street, *don't* forget your manners, *and don't* use bad language. Even in adulthood, we are inundated with "don'ts" regarding our behavior: *don't* say those words, *don't* wear those clothes, *don't* eat this, and *don't* touch that.

All of these "don'ts" form the boundaries of acceptable behavior. When reasonably imposed, boundaries are a necessary part of establishing appropriate and acceptable behavior. Manners, after all, are intended to make everyone comfortable, so that each person's dignity and feelings are safeguarded. All human groupings develop norms for behavior which each group member is expected to adhere to.

They vary in complexity and formality, but norms, boundaries, or "don'ts" are common. Of course, we can overdo boundary setting - when there are too many boundaries, it becomes a *tyranny*. In general, boundaries and standards of behavior ("manners") are necessary to the function of any human society.

What is generally left unsaid when establishing our group norms, is a target to focus on. It is not sufficient to merely describe the outside boundaries of the target, you also have to show people what the bullseye looks like. That's what this book is all about.

People can function in a world of "do's" and "don'ts," but knowing what to do and what not to do only describes external behavior. What people, particularly young people, really need is a vision of who we want them to *be*. With that vision, people are then empowered to reach *for* something rather than *avoiding* something.

To illustrate that point, imagine the following situation:

You are in a pitch black room with the task of finding a door somewhere in the room. What would you do? Most people would find the walls first, feeling their way slowly around the walls until they found the door, then opening the door to exit. But what if the exit was actually a trap door set in the floor? Or a staircase in the center of the room? What if there are no walls, or the walls gave way with pressure? Simply being told there is a door in the room isn't enough information to find the door. There is even less of a chance if the walls are unstable or missing.

Giving a person a vision of who we want them to be is like turning on an exit light in that imaginary room. The light will dimly illuminate the way, and give you a direction to walk toward. It could even be bright enough to illuminate the entire room.

What this thought experiment illustrates, is the need for both boundaries and a target: standards of behavior *and a positive vision* of who we want to be.

That's what I wanted to give those bright young Airmen at FTAC: a positive vision of who I want them to be. A vision of a person who is healthy, integrated, balanced and free - the kind of person who can be proud of who they are, as we are proud of them. I wanted to give them a vision to aim for, so they could grow into the kind of people others would want to follow.

And now I offer to you that same vision of whom I wanted them to be, and the kind of person I want to be as well.

Be Proud

Airmen take a lot of ribbing from our fellow warriors for the "soft" life Airmen they supposedly live compared to the other Services. It's not true, of course. Just like all modern warriors, Airmen work in a variety of environments ranging from pressurized cockpits at the threshold of space, to austere battlefields in far flung places, and of course air conditioned office as well. But the myth of the "easy" Air Force persists in some circles.

It's the same sort of stereotyping that happens within all of the Armed Services. Many a joke told in joint military commands begins with the opening line, "A Soldier, a Sailor, a Marine, and an Airman walk into a bar..." While it's fun to tease each other, trust me when I say that most Airmen don't spend their days playing golf, lounging by the pool, or punching keyboards in air conditioned offices. We are warriors, and we are proud of our Service, and proud to be part of the Joint Team.

When I faced those young Airmen coming into the Air Force, I wanted them to understand the organization they joined was not the caricature they might have heard about from family members or classmates at joint technical schools. Everyone should be proud of their Service, so I began the discussion about who I wanted them to be by telling them about the organization they'd joined.

> *You have joined the United States Air Force, the mightiest military force in the history of the planet. We can go anywhere on the planet we choose to go, and either look at it, feed it, or kill it. One Air Force bomber wing can devastate an entire country, and a single Air Force fighter plane can put a 2,000 pound weapon into a specific window of a specific building to destroy a specific target on order from the President. When Navy SEALS or Army Rangers get into trouble, they call Air Force gunships and pararescuemen to come to their aid. We fly in space; we command two-thirds of America's nuclear arsenal. Control of the ground and sea is contingent upon control of the air. The United States Air Force controls the air.*

> *We are part of a joint team, and each Service brings their own special skills and competencies to bear to defend*

America and her allies. We don't brag and we don't denigrate our joint teammates. Good natured ribbing is fine and even healthy, but never let friendly competition turn into running someone else down. Be proud to be an Airman, be proud of your teammates, and be proud of your contribution to the joint team.

It was a little bit of cheerleading for my own Service, of course, but the goal is to instill a sense of pride into these new Airmen. Being aware of the way we poke fun at each other in the military, my aim was to insulate those young people from becoming a self-fulfilling stereotype. I want and expect Airmen to be proud of the Air Force, as I want and expect Marines, Soldiers, and Sailors to be proud of their branches of the Service.

Being proud of who you are should not be confined to the wearing of a particular uniform; I believe everyone should take pride in who they are and what they are capable of becoming. While the genesis of "Be Proud" started with "Be Proud of Being an Airman," the principle extends to a broader perspective, "Be Proud of Who You Are."

Everyone Can Be Proud Of Something

The saddest people I have ever met were those who doubted their own self-worth. Sometimes because of their own poor choices, but more often because another person had beaten them down, the person without self-esteem looks in the mirror and sees nothing of value.

Experts on human behavior write volumes on how to increase our self-esteem or pride in oneself. Everyone has a theory about how to improve it. While there are plenty of gimmicks out there, the only true sense of self-worth is the one that grows from within, based on the real and potential gifts in a person. To put it another way, a person can repeat, "I'm good enough, I'm smart enough" to himself all day while continuing to be a doormat. No one can rely on external influences and gimmicks; each of us has to seize on something within ourselves. Even an *esprit de corps* expertly generated by a charismatic leader can only go so far... at some point each individual has to take their "team" pride and make it their own.

The purpose of *The Five Be's* is to help you be free and healthy so you can be the person *you* want to be.

Everyone has something they can be proud of, and their mentors and friends should encourage them to find those things within them. For some, it's their achievements and their relationships with others. For others, their sense of pride and self-worth comes from their relationships, or how they serve others. A person can be proud of their family, or their company's accomplishments; they can be proud of the mission of their company. The point is each person has *something* for which they can be proud. The task of mentors, parents, and leaders is to help individuals find their own strength by helping them find something that gives a sense of internal pride and self-worth.

Esprit de Corps

Before we begin the discussion on helping people find their own strengths, it is important to address the external aspects of "pride." In the military, as illustrated in my "Airman" speech to the FTAC Airmen, it is virtuous for individuals to subordinate their own needs to that of the group. The Air Force Core Value of *"Service Before Self" embodies this idea.* For mentors, coaches, and leaders in every type of organization, esprit de corps builds team cohesion and imparts a sense of belonging to the group. *Esprit de corps*, literally "spirit of the body", is the collective pride in the larger group. It is a necessary and desirable starting point used to assemble a group of people into a team to accomplish a shared goal.

Helping our new Airmen find some pride in their organization was the reason I began my speech to the FTAC Airmen the way I did. Reminding them about the might of the Service they volunteered to join. In order for the young Airmen to take their service seriously, they needed to take their Service seriously. *Esprit de corps* helps a person take pride in their group membership, enabling them to overcome the natural and human tendency of placing individual interests before the groups'.

Furthermore, the subordination of an individual's needs will assist that group member's personal growth. The principle is the same in many walks of life, such as athletics, religion, business or art. Any time we learn to delay gratification for the good of others, we gain the opportunity to learn something new about ourselves, and as a side effect, advanced the shared goals of the group.

Preparation + Opportunity
= Victory

This is pride experienced from group participation in the best case. Like all things, divergence to either extreme can create vice. In the extreme, if individuals twist pride into fanaticism. If pride in one's group results in the subordination of *all* good outside of the group then people become fanatics.

Fanatics are capable of great harm, either through violence or just plain ugliness. It is the same vice that generates bullying in high school and at its most extreme, war crimes like ethnic cleansing. On the other end of the scale, the wrong sort of pride in the group creates a user of people, where they spend their lives in subordination to the group to the exclusion of all other good. This is the kind of pride that generates the stereotypical "salaryman"[1] who neglects his family for work.

Therefore, mentors and leaders should appreciate the power of external motivation and *esprit de corps*, and use that power only for good... the good of the team *and* the good of the individual.

Esprit de corps should inspire us to achieve, to become virtuous, and to become better people.

Looking Inside for the Good

Externals influences are powerful, but they only go so far. At some point, people have to find meaning within themselves. Healthy people accomplish more personally and professionally. If we strive to raise healthy people; we must first help them find their own self-worth.

Each person, regardless of status, wealth, beauty, or even accomplishment has value because they are a unique human being with inherent self-worth. While an individual can distinguish himself by unique characteristics, each of us must never lose sight of the fact we have something to contribute. Sometimes we confuse "self-worth" with "self-esteem." .

It is useful to do some word analysis in order to clearly differentiate between the two concepts: "worth" and "esteem." The Oxford Dictionary defines "worth" and "esteem" as:

Worth: Sufficiently good, important, or interesting to justify a specified action; deserving to be treated or regarded in the way specified.

Esteem: Respect and admiration, typically for a person.

Do you see the difference? Your self-worth is inherent, while esteem depends on an opinion given by someone else. For example, an athlete can have very high self-worth, being a kind or generous person, but have very low esteem (self- or otherwise) for any number of reasons like harsh criticism. Your "self-worth" is *independent* of what others think of you, or even what you think of yourself – human beings have inherent worth.

Naturally, we understand the idea of the innate worth of a human being in general, but a great number of people have a difficulty understanding that *they* are valuable. We don't accept bullying, we demand equal pay for equal work, we rebel at unfair play in sports, and we are quick to defend the innocent or weak from harm. But somehow, we have a difficult time transferring that innate sense of another's worth, into accepting our own self-worth.

I recently saw a great television commercial produced by a popular soap manufacturer that perfectly illustrates the point of recognizing our own blind spots. In the commercial, the manufacturer asked several women to describe themselves to a forensic sketch artist. In their descriptions, the women proceeded to point out all of their flaws as part of the descriptive process.

After the women left the room, a second group entered the room, and proceeded to describe the first group of subjects. The members of the second group had just met the subjects, and had spent some time getting to know them. They pointed out the good things, such as "a nice smile" or "bright eyes". The subjects then returned to view the two drawings the artist had created.

The sketches the artists created using the women's self-descriptions were harsh and stark with little beauty. However, the portraits generated by the descriptions from others showed the women as they are seen by rest of the world – interesting and charismatic.

Self-worth, therefore, is not merely respecting yourself or accepting adulation from others. It is realizing that you have worth, because you are inherently equal in dignity to every other person. We are not all equal in rank, social status, looks or ability, but we are all equal in dignity. Recognizing that you have something to offer, no matter what it might be, and is recognition of your own inherent value.

Authentic Pride

Authentic pride should *never* tear someone down; rather, authentic pride is about carrying oneself with dignity while recognizing the same dignity in others.

Returning to the example I used with the Airmen; I reminded them that friendly ribbing between the military Services is good for morale and teamwork, but when that friendly ribbing turns mean-spirited, it becomes a problem. I call that "Counterfeit Pride." While being insistent on not allowing *others* to tear us down (or our teammates), we must refuse to follow suit. Our goal should never be to build ourselves up by tearing *them* down.

There is actually some science supporting the idea of "Authentic Pride" vs "Counterfeit Pride." In a 2007 study, University of British Columbia, Assistant Professor Jessica Tracy[2] and University of California Davis, Professor Richard Robins, found that authentic pride in oneself is a key component to well-being. In a two-year study conducted from 2003 to 2005 in rural Toussiana, Burkina Faso, Tracy showed photos of Americans and West Africans to

Burkinabe subjects who could neither read nor write. The test subjects then labeled each photo with a perceived emotion: anger, disgust, fear, happiness, sadness or surprise. Tracy discovered that there was a basic human ability, regardless of culture or education, to identify pride within the photos.

Furthermore, Tracy was able to distinguish two different types of pride: "Authentic" and "Huberistic." Authentic pride is the preferred type, pride in accomplishment, the shared pride of a championship sports team or making the Honor Roll. Authentic pride helps to reinforce self-worth and promotes confidence, and a yearning to strive for greater achievement.

"Huberistic" pride, or "counterfeit", as I call it, is just the opposite. It drags others down causing interpersonal conflict. Counterfeit pride contributes to an inflated ego, and prevents an individual from having authentic self-worth.

In Hawaii, there two types of crabs that could be used as the "poster crabs" for pride. A bucket full of A'ama Crabs will fight over each other to climb out, pushing and shoving each other to gain an escape advantage. As soon as one crab starts to get out of the bucket, another will pull him back in. None of the crabs are able to escape the bucket.

Be like the Alamihi Crab, not
the A'ama Crab!

- Hawaiian Proverb

The Alamihi Crab is different. They will actually build a ladder from their own bodies, and *pull each other out*. That's what authentic pride - real self-worth - does for us. It not only builds our own confidence, it actually builds up others too. Be an Alamihi Crab!

Be Free

"Freedom" is a word often misused in our current vocabulary. We view our "freedoms" in such a broad manner that the word sometimes loses its meaning. Particularly in the case of young people, "freedom" is synonymous with "doing whatever I like", but that's not authentic freedom. Authentic freedom is being able to choose what's good for you, and yet remaining unencumbered by things that prevent you from being healthy. In fact, unbounded freedom to do whatever I want whenever I want is not freedom; it is license.

It's really not a radical concept, the idea that freedom is bound by responsibilities and limits; in fact it's preserved in our system of laws and our notion of justice. We regulate speech and assembly both for the common good and for the individual's good. People are not permitted to gather for the purpose of fomenting violence, and we don't allow a person to run into a theater and shout "fire" without just cause. Ideally, our laws are constructed to both protect the common good, and safeguard individual liberty. However, the freedom we enjoy as Americans is not unfettered liberty. We are free but we do not have license to do whatever we want.

> *For to be free is not merely to*
> *cast off one's chains, but to live*
> *in a way that respects and*
> *enhances the freedom of others.*

> *- Nelson Mandela*

Authentic freedom is an individual's ability to choose what is good without being impeded or bound, be it an internal or external restriction. If an individual's appetites or another person's demands prevent the individual from making good choices, then we can objectively say that the individual is not free.

For example, if a person is addicted to a behavior or substance, then the addiction is ruling the person's life, not freedom of choice. The extreme example of course is drug abuse, but there are many more things that can control someone's life, preventing them from choosing what's best for them. Overeating will keep a person from exercising properly and maintaining physical health; working excessive hours will limit interaction with family and friends; viewing pornography debases a person's view on sex and damages relationships, etc. When it comes to vice and addictions, there are literally "a million of them" out there. To sum it up, if your appetites control you, then you are not free.

Addiction is a massive world-wide problem, with millions bound to some "force" other than the ability to choose what's best for them. According to a 2014 report by the U.S. Department of Health and Human Services[3], addiction to tobacco, alcohol, and illicit drugs cost $700 million in health care. In 2012, 4.3 million Americans met the clinical criteria for dependence or abuse of marijuana in the previous year.[4]

Drug and alcohol dependence are easy targets and well known, but what about other addictions? In a 2008 University of Pittsburgh study, 9% of the 3,034 participants showed signs of video game addiction[5,6] Debt can be similarly crushing to our freedom. In 2015, the Federal Reserve reported Americans owe a whopping $3.34 trillion in consumer debt. If people are depending on high interest loans or being forced to make certain choices because of their debt, can we truly say they are free?

Societal expenses such as health care are not the only costs to surrendering your freedom. Addiction requires personal costs, as well. People who suffer from addictions report that their addictions control their day to day activities and actions restricting the ability to think or act on any impulse except obtaining the next fix. Many of these unfortunate people end up abandoning their family, careers, friends, and even their homes due to the overriding addiction. I don't think anyone would disagree that someone who's addicted is not free.

This is such a problem that we have an entire industry dedicated to helping people overcome addictions. There are thousands of addiction rehabilitation programs throughout the country – from the usual addictions like drugs and alcohol to internet and video game addiction. The common theme is that something becomes a problem when it takes command of a person's life.

Note, I use the terms "demands" or "appetites" here with the implication they are unreasonable or unhealthy. That's not to be confused with having rules or even laws that govern behavior. Rules do not make a person fettered, in fact, we need rules to help maintain our freedom. I know that sounds backwards, but let me give you two examples.

First, consider the case of gravity. At first, it would seem that gravity is something that holds us bound and restricts our movement. However, gravity is actually the reason we have physical freedom of movement. We begin with some basic physics – all objects with mass have gravity, and everything in the Universe is in motion. Therefore, the sun, Earth, even your own body have some measure of gravity. According to Newton's Laws of Motion, an object at rest or in motion won't change its direction or speed unless something acts on it. Imagine an astronaut suddenly appears in a universe with no gravity (laws). Without the "Law" of gravity, our poor astronaut would be stuck traveling in whatever direction he happened to be traveling when he appeared, or stuck wherever he happened to be, until he collides with something. However, in a Universe with a "Law" of gravity, we have the freedom to move where we like and can even use gravity to assist us in traveling through space by using gravity to accelerate spacecraft around planets. Without gravity, there is no freedom. What was originally perceived as a constraint of freedom has actually been an enabler of freedom from the beginning.

For the second example, we will look at traffic controls which are tools such as traffic signals, signage, speed limits, and pavement markings. Traffic controls restrict the flow of vehicular traffic on roads and highways to comply with specific safety rules and guidelines. A superficial look at traffic controls would imply that traffic controls restrict a driver's freedom, but the opposite is actually the case. Imagine how dangerous roads would be without speed limits, signage or lane markings.

*What fascinates me about addiction
and obsessive behavior is that
people would choose an altered
state of consciousness that's toxic
and ostensibly destroys most
aspects of your normal life, because
for a brief moment you feel okay.*

- *Moby, musician-songwriter*

However, with appropriate traffic controls, we have the freedom to safely travel wherever we like. We can feel safe travelling at high speeds on the highway since we know that our fellow motorists will also be following the guidelines ensuring safe travel for all. Appropriate behavioral controls permit us to remain free, and in this case unharmed.

The opposite of freedom is not "just" confinement or restriction. As we will discuss in the next section, Aristotle's philosophy of the Golden Mean, is that virtue lies in the middle between the extremes of vice.

Therefore, on one end of the "freedom continuum" lies *slavery*, and on the other lies *license*. Just as slavery is the abuse of freedom to hold another unjustly bound, license likewise is an abuse of freedom since it binds our own will to our appetites or passions. The newspaper is brimming with stories of people who abused their own freedom either through the self-abuse or by allowing others to abuse them. "Excessive freedom" is as much a problem as a complete lack of freedom, and in fact ends up in the same place: slavery. On the ends of the "freedom continuum" is slavery to others and slavery to appetites – both are self-destructive.

As a military officer, I often remind my Airmen that the Air Force doesn't set standards of behavior to hinder their freedom (i.e., regulations). Rather, we set standards of behavior to keep them safe and healthy, ready to accomplish our mission – to have the defense of our countrymen in our hands is a serious responsibility.

When Airmen violate these standards, leaders must do their duty and hold them accountable – this is justice. Furthermore, being held accountable is actually *good* for morale. The consequences for violating military standards range from minor to severe, depending on the seriousness of the offense, and always entails some sort of penalty such as a fine, extra duty, or demotion of rank. When others see an offender receive their just deserts for violating the rules or the law, it reinforces their confidence in their leaders and each other.

To summarize, true freedom does not come at someone else's expense and true freedom doesn't result from selfishness or self-centeredness. True freedom comes from serving others and respecting both our own and others' dignity. True freedom enables us to grow as human persons.

Be Virtuous

When someone uses the word "virtue", we immediately form a mental picture of a saint or an unattainable standard, but that need not be so. "Virtue" is not necessarily the sole domain of religion or any particular religion or moral philosophy followers of religion, nor should its association with religion create a barrier to adopting "virtue" as a "Be."

It's helpful to examine the common critiques up front. Critics of the idea of "virtue" as a realistic, achievable standard, of behavior dismiss the idea humans have the innate ability to live virtuous lives. It would be naive to ignore the terrible offenses people commit against others and society, but the opposite is also true. There are just as many stories of valor, love, self-sacrifice, and generosity in the world as well. People are capable of great evil, but we are also capable of great virtue.

We know from observing the world that both are true, that evil and good coexist within humanity, and so it makes sense that an admirable goal is to cultivate the good and weed out the bad in ourselves. When we nurture the goodness in ourselves and others. We call that goodness "virtue".

Every culture, community, and religion has its own idea of what virtue means. For example, in the US Air Force, we define "virtue" as adhering to the Core Values, *"Integrity first"*, *"Service before self"*, and *"Excellence in all we do"*. As an institution, the Air Force considers an Airman "virtuous" if he lives by the Core Values,

We can trace our modern concept of virtue back to the classical Greek civilization of in the 4th Century BC and the famous philosopher, Aristotle. He defined the classical ideal and what has become known as the "Cardinal Virtues." The word "cardinal" refers to the "principle" or "main" virtues, much like North, South, East, and West are the "Cardinal Directions" on a compass.

Aristotle's idea was that the highest calling was living a virtuous life, which perfected a person in the eyes of the gods, as well as in the eyes of his fellow man. These ideas became so central to Western culture, that years later when Christianity became dominant in political and philosophical thought in the Roman Empire, other philosophers like Augustine and Aquinas "baptized" the ideal of Classical Virtue and then added their own Christian-specific virtues called the Theological Virtues.

The Greek philosophers Aristotle and Plato both agreed that virtue begins with the understanding of what the medieval philosopher Aquinas later called "first principles." First principles are the "universal human goods" that all humans aspire to and recognize as admirable. Aristotle's list included: life, beauty, love, truth, creativity, religion, and sociability. The virtuous person protects and seeks to increase these universal human goods, while the imprudent person squanders them. While we probably rarely use the words "virtuous" and "vice" in everyday speech, we have all seen people whose choices we questioned. Social media and the paparazzi thrive on highlighting behavior that makes us wonder, "What were they thinking?" When someone gets in trouble or makes choices that harm their reputation, or others, those choices are usually a direct result of someone not exercising a virtue. In fact, we don't need a specific belief system or code of ethics to understand what's right or wrong--although they certainly help as guides!----those Universal Human Goods are written into our psyche.

For example: we know that defacing a natural monument or someone else's property with graffiti is wrong because it disturbs our sense of Beauty. We know betrayal of a loved one is wrong because it violates our sense of Loyalty. In addition, we know that lying to someone to cover up a crime is wrong, since it violates both Truth.

The Cardinal Virtues, sometimes also known as the Classical Virtues are the means which humans defend Universal Human Goods, our own humanity, and the health of society. The Cardinal Virtues are prudence, justice, temperance, and fortitude. We will go over each of these, one at a time.

Prudence

Prudence is the ability for one to determine what is appropriate at any given time.

In the virtue of Prudence, we find the ability to make sound choices in the real world – choices that either expose us and others to danger or shield us from it.

Having Prudence does not need to be a "weighty" way to live -- it can be as simple as having good manners. When the choices are clear, then Prudence is an easy virtue.

For example, we all know serious acts, such as taking the life of an innocent person or stealing property are morally wrong. Only a sociopath would have difficulty discerning right from wrong in those extreme circumstances. Most daily choices aren't that clear cut. Friends sometimes put us in awkward positions by making questionable choices expecting us to approve or even go along. Other times people misbehave and when they get away with it without penalty, it might cause us to question our own internal moral compass. Advice columnists make a very good living writing answers to the daily moral dilemmas that ordinary people face in their lives.

However, most of us don't have the luxury of clear cut choices. We tell "white lies" to avoid hurting someone's feelings. Perhaps we sneak away after we bump someone's car and hope they don't notice the dent. These are everyday opportunities to increase our virtue if we truly value Truth, or become a little less human if we don't.

The character that takes command in moments of crucial choices has already been determined. It has been determined by a thousand other choices made earlier in seemingly unimportant moments... the decisions that, piece by piece, bit by bit, developed... habits of duty and honor and integrity—or dishonor and shame.

- Ronald Reagan, U.S. President

A personal story might be helpful here, as it illustrates a lack of prudence that could have cost me my life, and how the common choices we make sometimes have profound consequences.

My college friends and I were inner-tubing down the Guadalupe River near San Antonio, Texas and came upon the spot known as the "Blue Hole." It was a very deep spot in the river, and is probably connected to a subterranean aquifer. It was a local tradition for people to leap from an overhanging rock face into the Blue Hole. My initial answer to the invitation was, "No, thank you". However, once the boys swam away, leaving me alone with all the girls, my testosterone got the better of me and I raced to join them. I had a couple of chances to back out, including looking over the 20-foot drop-off, down to the water below. I didn't use the proper judgment – I wasn't prudent enough to back out even though I *really* did not want to jump.

My companions counted to three and we all stepped off the precipice – I instantly regretted my decision. "*This was a dumb idea,*" I thought as I plummeted to the water below, along with six other boys, all within an arms' reach of each other. We hit the water so hard, and I went so deep that I nearly ran out of air before I made it back to the surface. There were a hundred things that could have gone wrong, and we were very lucky that no one was hurt. That experience was a great lesson in Prudence for me – that I should listen to my inner voice when it is shouting at me to pay attention

There are other ways to demonstrate Prudence besides deciding not to jump off 20-foot high rocks. The virtue of Prudence is also helpful when making ordinary decisions, such as what to eat for dinner, or whether to accelerate through a yellow traffic light (or not). In fact, it's the daily small choices that define us far ***more than the big ones.***

An *imprudent* person usually becomes that way through the accumulation of seemingly small choices over a period of time. The person with the lead foot has learned they can get away with driving as if they're on a race course because they have done it often enough for the habit to form. However, most people learn quickly, either through their own mistakes or someone else's, that refusal to obey traffic laws will result in speeding tickets, a wrecked car, or worse. These days, texting while driving is a far bigger problem than "merely" speeding. Prudent drivers put the phone away, imprudent ones attempt to operate a three ton automobile with only one hand and one eye at high speed.

In short, I believe human beings innately understand the idea of "Universal Human Goods", which is why there are some commonalities in moral standards regardless of upbringing or religious tradition. It is also why Prudence is a virtue that is both achievable and universal.

Justice

Justice is the proper moderation between self-interest, the rights and needs of others, and rendering to each person what is deserved.

We most often think of "Justice in the legal sense: the system of enforcement of laws, including punishment for committing crimes. But the virtue of Justice is much more than merely administering laws and regulations. At a basic level, the essence of justice is that people are given their due. There is a measure of precision in Justice, because to do so requires a person to weigh and measure what another deserves. Unlike the other three virtues which deal primarily with self-governing, Justice is a virtue that applies to how we treat others.

How does the ordinary person employ the virtue of Justice? Is Justice only for courts and police? Of course not.

Like all the virtues, the ordinary person can develop the virtue of Justice by treating others fairly in their common dealings. Paying a fair price for what you buy is Justice, as is repaying a loan promptly and in full. Taking responsibility for a failure in the workplace and not allowing another to take the blame is also a form of Justice. In fact, we have the opportunity to apply Justice in all of our personal, professional and familial relationships. Justice need not have a negative connotation, such as "bringing a criminal to Justice." It can, and should be, a positive virtue where we understand and willingly accept our responsibilities to others.

Like all virtues, we can abuse Justice as well. If we weigh competing needs unequally, or a person's application or desire for Justice overwhelms Universal Human Good (such as Truth), then Justice can easily transform into the vices *vengeance* or *lawlessness*. Justice as a virtue is not an end in and of itself – it is a means where we, as individuals and as a society, protect human dignity.

Justice's other traveling companion is Mercy. Mercy allows us to temper raw justice so we respect Universal Human Goods and inflict no unnecessary harm in the name of Justice. For example, in many countries, automobile operators are considered "professional drivers" and are *criminally liable* for vehicular accidents. Justice demands criminal sanction in some cases, but Mercy applied by those in authority, when appropriate, prevents people from going to jail for routine "fender benders". Raw Justice would fill jails, Mercy ensures only actual criminals go there.

Temperance

Temperance is the practice of self-control, moderation and abstinence.

Whenever we think of the word "Temperance," many probably think of Carrie Nation and Prohibition. While moderation or even abstention from alcohol can be Temperance, it is actually a narrow view of it as a virtue. Temperance applies to keeping competing appetites in balance, similar to the way high achieving athletes and scholars train their minds and bodies. In a few words, Temperance means governing your natural human appetites in a way that preserves freedom and prevents harm.

Researchers found that children with who practice good self-control, (i.e., typically better at paying attention, persist with difficult tasks, and suppress inappropriate or impulsive behaviors), are much more likely to find and retain employment as adults, spending 40% less time unemployed than those with a lower capacity for self-control.[7]

"All things in moderation" is a common phrase to describe Temperance., and it works in general, For example, an occasional glass of wine with dinner is fine and even thought to be healthy by some researchers. However, habitual excessive drinking is destructive to the body and relationships. Food is necessary for life, and good food is a pleasure – overindulging or eating unhealthy food intentionally is destructive. Even the internet and video games can be transformed from a fun activity or useful tool into soul crushing addictions if we allow it.

Temperance is the exercise of the will, to enjoy what's good without letting it become an addiction. It does not need to be one of the "common" vices, simple unhealthy attachment to things can become personally destructive.

For example, take the attachment to "things". Moving as often as I have during my military career, my family has had the unique opportunity to eliminate a lot of 'stuff'. We have been fairly successful at paring our belongings down to a necessary minimum, mostly voluntarily but sometimes involuntarily, when things are lost or broken during shipment. Consequently, there are very few things that are truly precious to any of us, and the items that are precious to us have sentimental rather than monetary value. Each time movers (strangers) have come to my home to box up our household and then load everything onto a truck, we have to come to grips with what is really important. We hold our breath and entrust those same strangers to deliver everything we possess to a new house, a new assignment. When the house is empty and the papers are signed, watching the truck drive away forces me to remember that "it's only stuff". Each time in this situation, my family is offered the opportunity to practice a little Temperance.

The polar opposite example of Temperance with our "stuff" is hoarding. You might be familiar with the television show that is similarly named. The people the cast and producers are trying to help, have let "stuff" completely take over their lives. By allowing their homes to overflow with possessions (and debris), they often forfeited relationships with family and friends, and frequently endangered their own health. Without Temperance and the ability to prioritize appropriately, competing appetites will control us until we are no longer free. Without Temperance, our own appetites and passions can enslave us and cause us harm.

Athletes understand this virtue very well, as they discipline their minds and bodies in order to achieve success in their sport. They may take on a special or restrictive diet, they may trade sleep for workouts, and they eschew certain celebrations, or even common comforts, in order to be their best. This sort of mental, physical, and spiritual preparation is a commonly proven way for athletes to succeed. We applaud that sort of self-control in them, but is it really out of reach for us?

Of course not. We all have practice applying Temperance, at a variety of levels. I believe the virtue of Temperance, applied in a sensible way that respects Universal Human Goods, is a necessary component to living a healthy adult life. Whenever we delay gratification or order our priorities toward a specific end, we are practicing Temperance. So, when we stay late to finish the presentation that is due tomorrow, we are subsuming our own personal comfort because others are counting on us. When we make sure to leave on time to meet our spouse for dinner, we are balancing our time for the spouse we vowed to "love, honor, and cherish". When we decline dessert so we can stick to our diet, when we turn off *Call of Duty* to help our kids with their homework, and when we delay our lunch to comfort a coworker having a bad day – those are demonstrations of te Temperance.

Let Carrie Nation bury the hatchet, those of us with a balanced sense of Temperance will continue to grow and become "more free" by gaining an ability to control our own appetites.

Fortitude

Fortitude is defined as the forbearance, endurance, and ability to confront fear and uncertainty, or intimidation.

Of all of the Cardinal Virtues, I think that fortitude is the easiest to understand.

When you have the virtue of Fortitude, you have the ability to see through the trials and tribulations of a task to the end goal, and the patience to endure the discomfort, or even danger that may accompany those trials. We value Fortitude highly in all occupations and walks of life and occupations, from those requiring physical labor to students "burning the midnight oil" in order to earn a diploma. Fortitude is merely the strength to endure hardship.

Every trial endured and weathered
in the right spirit makes a soul
nobler and stronger than it was
before.
–James Buckham

In many professions and pursuits, leaders use hard work and even hardship as a tool to train individuals and teams to have self-confidence so they can achieve. The military uses shared hardship (restrictions on freedom and physical exercise) as a training tool in basic training with the specific purpose of creating a bond among the recruits. People often bond when they share and survive a tough experience. They also learn something in the experience as well: they learn they can "take" more than perhaps they originally thought they could. The same is true for an athlete; hard training improves an athlete's perception of what can be endured. They learn to adapt to the pain and stress of competition.

Military service and athletes serve as useful examples, but what about the rest of humanity not preparing for combat or the Super Bowl? Fortitude is important for the "every day person" since hardship is a part of ordinary life. Ordinary trials such as a new parent's sleep deprivation, cleaning up after a sick child, or pulling an 'all-nighter' for a school project are all examples of when an ordinary person needs to exhibit fortitude.

We develop Fortitude like we develop other virtues, through the daily choices made on seemingly insignificant issues that over time strengthen our constitution.

There's an old adage in military training that's apropos: *"In combat, no one rises to the occasion, they sink to the level of their training"*, which means that during stressful times or crises, we all revert to the way we have lived until that point. No one can discover the strength needed to endure a trial if they haven't suffered and endured trials in the past. This is the true reason self-denial is beneficial; it provides us with the training needed to make the best possible decisions during stressful situations rather than allowing situations or others to dictate what happens to us.

Virtue does not need to be feared. I hope that you can see that authentic virtue is an achievable and even desirable goal. By safeguarding the Universal Human Goods through virtuous behavior, we improve ourselves and those around us. Virtuous people make their teams better, and those around them better, and they achieve more. Truly virtuous people can improve civilization.

Be Balanced

When my son was very young, he would give me the same advice as I left for work each day: *"Goodbye, Daddy, have a good day at work. Be sure to drink your water, eat your lunch, and make new friends."* Without realizing it, my son was encouraging me to live a balanced life. I always thought his farewell each day was far more insightful than just a small boy's simple advice. In fact, it's a great way to think about life balance.

There are many different ways to understand and dissect the topic of life balance. My model consists of 3 main focus areas: *Body, Mind,* and *Spirit.* Others use *Health, Wealth,* and *Friends,* or *Work/Life.* The US Air Force has an outstanding approach to balancing the demands of work and life in their *Comprehensive Airman Fitness Model* which takes the familiar *Mental, Physical,* and *Spiritual* dimensions and adds a fourth, *Social.* Additionally, there's the familiar Maslow's 'Hierarchy of Needs' (Figure 1).

Figure 1. Maslow's hierarchy of needs (1943)

No matter how you slice up the facets of the human person, the takeaway is that humans *are* multi-dimensional. Therefore, we all should be deliberate about developing our whole person and not just one aspect. Each person has a body, mind, and the intangible part of themselves called a soul or human spirit. There is more to every person than meets the eye.

Being a well rounded person means trying to determine what motivates and fulfills you, and then intentionally working to harmonize those very personal needs with the needs of your family, team, or workplace. It's more than a mere transaction; leaders must recognize that their team is more than names on an organizational chart. Each is a person with needs and aspirations of their own, who have come together to do a job for their own reasons. As individuals, we need to understand our personal engagement with those around us is just as important as our self-awareness.

The companies consistently rated 'best to work for' seem to understand that idea. Those companies provide benefits that let the employees know they are valued for more than just their contribution to the bottom line, but also valued as people. In each case, the employees at the top rated companies enjoy their work environment; the benefits provided are a bonus. The companies that treat their employees as whole persons, with more than a single dimension, are the ones who get the most engaged and involved employees, in return.

> *I believe that being successful means
> having a balance [in] life. You can't
> truly be considered successful in your
> business life if your home life is in
> shambles.*
>
> *– Zig Ziglar*

The next time you look at yourself in the mirror, stop for a minute and remember the words of my then four year old son: *"drink your water, eat your lunch, and make new friends."*

Living life balance is challenging. There are a lot of demands on a person's time: work, family, friends, hobbies, etc., and finding time to feed all aspects of the body and soul is key to any successful life. Anyone can put their head down and power through life, however, it takes a mature person to understand that how you live is equally important as what you accomplish. Keeping our lives in balance and living an integrated life is important to everyone.

To have a discussion about life balance, we must have something to balance. Thinking about the human person in three categories provides a way to examine how to keep things in balance – and what will happen when we are unbalanced.

Humans are complex creatures that can be categorized in a number of ways. It's fair to say that each field of study, scientific or philosophical, has a unique way of looking at the human person. This is necessary since attempts to synthesize all areas of study for humans is *very* complex work! I think that it is important to accept the underpinnings of the model before we begin tinkering with it.

The Human in Three Parts

"*Be Balanced*" refers to keeping all aspects of the human person in the proper perspective. There are many different models of human beings, from various personality and physical models to more esoteric ones. A common way to think about humans is to view each one as a composite of body, mind, and spirit. That is the model I will use to analyze life balance as a concept.

The first component of the human person is the Body, and it is where most people begin when getting to know someone. We will begin there. Bodies come in great variety: long, tall, short, round, male, female, and an almost endless assortment of skin colors. The biological definition of a person is the easiest, despite its multitude of categories, since the various characteristics that define a person's appearance, sound, and smell are available to us without any sort of intimacy.

We can feel another person using our senses without actually getting to know the person. Physicians, dietitians, physical therapists, workout trainers, and coaches all focus on the development and care of our bodies. Scientists classify the various branches of humanity through physical appearance: i.e., *homo sapiens* are distinctly different than *homo erectus*. Let us establish that one component of the human person is the *Body*.

The second component of the human person is the Mind. Intuitively, we know we are more than just the sum of our physical parts. The philosophical maxim, *Cognito, ergo sum* (I think, therefore I am) is a testament to that intuition.

Since you are reading these words and processing them using the knowledge and experience that you have obtained through life experiences, you are validating that philosophical maxim. In addition to the biological and medical fields of study, we also have several areas of study dedicated to understanding the workings of the human mind. While psychologists are interested in the physiology of the brain, they are also interested in the study of the *Mind*.

The Mind is more than merely the electrochemical exchanges that take place in the brain. If that's all there was, it would be *instinct* rather than *reason* – "brain" rather than "mind." However, humans have the ability to reason, to retain information, to process and combine that information in new ways that enables further development. Our brains don't get physically larger, but our minds are constantly increasing in capacity as new information is absorbed and processed. Due to this demonstrated ability to process thoughts, data, and to learn, we can establish the second part of our human model, the *Mind*.

The third component of the human person is the Spirit. Are humans just thinking machines able to do calculus *and* also able to lift rocks? I submit we are far more than thinking machines. We have a Human Spirit. To clarify, this is not about religion or even spirituality, although religion and spirituality are the Human Spirit seeking something greater than itself. This is the Human Spirit referenced as the human condition. Whether or not you are a person with religious beliefs, you believe in the Human Spirit--and I can prove it. Read on.

While we cannot physically observe the Human Spirit, we can view its effects and feel its presence in what medieval

philosopher and theologian Thomas
Aquinas named the 'Universal Human
Goods'. Aquinas' idea is ancient, and
springs from both Greek philosophy and the
work of 5th century theologian and
philosopher St. Augustine of Hippo.

"Universal Human Goods" are
spiritual goods every human can relate to,
regardless of whether you are a person of
faith or no faith at all. "Universal Human
Goods" are concepts such as Truth, Beauty,
and Love. As humans with an immortal
soul, we experience *love* for people and
ideals, we delight in the *beauty* found in
nature and art, and we demand and respect
truth. While there isn't a definitive list of
"Universal Human Goods", the basics of
truth, beauty, and *love* are sufficient to
emphasize the argument that humans are
more than mere flesh and blood.

Even the simplest of creatures can
feel emotions, but only humans can feel
Love with a "Capital L" in all its forms –
from "brotherly love" to "erotic love" to
"self-sacrificing love". *Beauty* is similar.
Animals, plants, or even geology, can form
beautiful things, simply as a byproduct of
their existence. Only humans can create

beauty Furthermore, not only do humans create beauty for its own sake, but we also appreciate the beauty in nature. Humans seek out *beauty* in nature, art, each other, and celebrate that *beauty,* each in our own way.

As humans, we seem to have an innate appreciation for Truth as a "good" to be preserved. Despite the fact that humans can and do lie to each other, I have yet to meet a person of any sort who thinks that lying is a "good." A lie is sometimes necessary, but most people will go to great lengths to avoid lying for any reason.

While it is true that we can fabricate all sorts of reasons for humans to be truthful or to create beautiful things, it is also true that those things are not generated strictly from our intellect.

Truth, beauty, and *love* all come from the wellspring of the Human Soul, that immortal and spiritual *essence* that makes us, "us". Various efforts to scientifically analyze the Human Spirit has only gone so far – scientists have been able to measure the weight of the human soul by weighing people before and after they die! All that being said, it should be obvious that if you have ever experienced *love* or *beauty*, clearly that appreciation came from a less tangible source than simply the brain or hormones—it came from your Human *Spirit*. Therefore, assembling all these "knowns" into a model, gives us Figure 2 below.

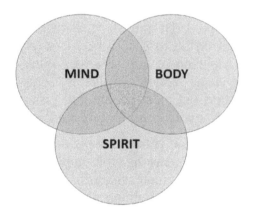

Figure 2. A Model of the Human Person as relationship of Mind, Body, and Spirit

Much is written about the need for "life balance" and "work-life balance,", but why should anyone "Be Balanced"? I propose that people are healthier and happier when we maintain a good balance of *body, mind*, and *spirit*; and we grow when we cultivate all three.

Consider the amount of time Americans spend at work. According to D.S. Hamermesh and E. Stancanelli's 2014 paper entitled *Long Workweeks and Strange Hours*[8], it was found Americans tend to work longer hours and more "off" hours (such as weekends and evening). Does this sound like "balance" to you? Certainly, there are times when we need to work long hours in order to complete a project or do satisfy a customer's requests, but when almost a third of all Americans are routinely working weekends – more than any other developed Western country – then something is out of balance. Sometimes it is easier to see when something is missing. So, what happens when we're not in balance?

The Body: The "Fitness Freak" and the "Couch Potato"

We only get one body, so we have to take care of it. Can you go too far? Sure you can. If you are devoting *all* of your energy to enhancing your physique, with none left over for anything else, you are likely out of balance. I'm not taking about professional and Olympic athletes who spend a great deal of time staying in top physical shape. Clearly, those people are making short term sacrifices for long term goals and rewards. But even professional football players and Olympians make time for friends and family. They also make time to 'recharge' by doing something else. Furthermore, professional athletes are also students of nutrition, physiology, and psychology, and incorporate that knowledge with their physical training.

This is not the case with the "Fitness Freak". The out of balance "Fitness Freak" is not able to find the energy or time for *anything* else in their lives. Their entire self-worth is wrapped up in their appearance, performance, or both. These people are most likely the ones posting selfies constantly ("look at me!") or skipping out on a great experience because they cannot prioritize properly.

The "Fitness Freak" steers clear of relationships, because it consumes time "better spent" at the gym. These are people that are often thought of as "shallow" or one-dimensional. Aside from the spectacular exceptions, the "Fitness Freak's" goal of perpetual youth are short-lived and eventually must fade as their body's natural aging progresses.

In the extreme, the "Fitness Freak" can fall victim to all manner of self-destructive fad diets or even abuse drugs and supplements that promise fast results, but instead deliver destruction to the body the Freak is attempting to perpetually maintain. It should not take much convincing to see that as a poor way to live.

If the "Fitness Freak's" single minded focus on the body is damaging, what about the other end of the spectrum – the "Couch Potato"? This is the person that doesn't exercise, eat properly, or get enough sleep. The Couch Potato will eventually lose their ability to engage in life. The lack of physical energy leads to emotional and spiritual energy drain, becoming an ever descending spiral of self-destruction, if a significant behavioral change is not made.

According to the World Health Organization (WHO), the "Couch Potato's" sedentary lifestyle significantly contributes to obesity, heart disease, loss of bone density, and eating disorders.[9] It is of such significance, that the WHO issued a health warning against the "Couch Potato" lifestyle, listing it as one of the ten most significant health risks in today's culture.

The "Couch Potato" doesn't even have the (short-lived) benefits of the Fitness Freak's fit appearance. As the "Couch Potato's" appearance slowly fades, they will withdraw further from life as they become less attractive to members of the opposite sex. As the slide into physical mediocrity increases, it becomes even more difficult for the "Couch Potato" to pull out of the dive and make a life change. At some point only super-human effort can enable the "Couch Potato" to reengage in life and start to live a balanced life.

What does a "Body in Balance" look like? As described with the various virtues, there can be a healthy compromise between the extremes of the "Couch Potato" and the "Fitness Freak." We should strive to be healthy, make a conscious effort to eat right (most of the time), exercise appropriately for our level of ability, and improve ourselves physically. It doesn't mean we have to be athletes, but it does mean that we need to take care of the only body we will ever have.

The Body Balanced person doesn't let their pursuit of health become a barrier to relationship. They engage with others, creating and maintaining bonds with family and friends, while keeping their passions in the proper context. The healthy person understands the connection between their body and the other elements of their person, preserving balance. A person with their body in balance is not afraid to have a piece of birthday cake, and is always encouraging others to engage in life. These are the people who not only stop to smell the roses, but also know where to *find* the roses in the garden.

The Mind: The "Bookworm" and the "Anti-Intellectual"

The "Bookworm" has a lot in common with "Yoda". Similar to the person with a bloated or anemic Human Spirit lives in a parallel universe with no "worldly" concerns, the person who spends all of their time improving their *Mind,* to the exclusion of all else, lives strictly in their own head. While expanding the mind following intellectual pursuits is certainly good for an individual, as well as society, there has to be more to life than books and lectures. Balanced people do not live their entire lives in the world of the mind.

The stereotype of a person who lives in their head often said to lack "common sense". The "Bookworm" knows only the theory and none of the practical application. While the Bookworm might know the principles behind the operation of an internal combustion engine, he probably would not know how to fix one. The "Bookworm" is often not comfortable with common human interaction, instead favoring books and spreadsheets, while posting online about fictional characters, rather than getting to know the cute girl sitting at the next desk. The "Bookworm" misses out on real life because they are too busy living in a fantasy world that they are reading about.

Don't confuse me with the facts, my mind is made up!

- The Anti-Intellectual

The "Anti-Intellectual" is the polar opposite of the Bookworm. They won't think in depth at all. The "Anti-Intellectual" sees no value in learning *anything* from books (or perhaps anything at all). The "Anti-Intellectual" actively scorns education as frivolous and a waste, claiming that intellectuals have no value. There is absolutely no room for discussion with an "Anti-Intellectual". Once an idea is stored away in that steel trap of a closed mind, no amount of facts will change their opinion. They listen to the same music, watch the same/similar television programs and only read material with the same viewpoint. If you have ever attempted to have a discussion on *anything* serious on Facebook, then you have probably met the

"Anti-Intellectual". Even sports analysis can get testy on social media!

> *"I'll never retire as long as I live – that's like retiring from life! I'll never stop writing, teaching, lecturing. If you're in good health, living is exciting on its own."*
>
> *- Bel Kaufman, 101 years*

How does an *in-balance* Mind look like? They are alive, and they are attractive to others because of the way their life shines with energy and joy. A person with a healthy mind is willing to learn new things throughout their entire life. Many educational institutions aspire to develop life-long love of learning in their students. When reporters ask those who have lived exceptionally long lives, what is their secret to reaching 90 or 100 years, many will say keeping their mind active is one of the most important factors. A person who keeps their Mind in balance, makes learning a priority, rather than an obsession. We have to feed our Mind good things, in the same way we feed our Human Spirit and Body. Learn a language, read something new, go see a movie, talk to someone you don't know – these are just a few ways to help your mind grow. I find writing and travel to be two of my most effective tools for exercising my mind. Find a way that speaks to you.

Every summer, my mother would take my brother and me down to the local community center to pick out a summer activity. Sometimes it was art lessons, other times it was a physical skill such as archery or basketball. In each case, our mother wanted to be sure we engaged our Minds over the summer break and she was right to do so. She instilled in us a desire for life-long learning and curiosity about what was going on around us.

That's the strength of having a balanced and engaged mind: you develop a zest for life and both curiosity and a stronger connection to the world around you. The trick to having a healthy mind is to use it, realizing that you have to engage in *life* instead of just thinking about it!

The Spirit: The "Cloud Dweller" and the "Starving Soul"

Just like with the Mind and the Body, the Spirit is balanced between extremes. The "Cloud Dweller" is someone who has overfed their Spirit, living elsewhere while their body walks around on Earth. The "Starving Soul" refuses to attend to their Spirit.

When I talk about someone who is over-feeding their Human Spirit, I'm *not* talking about someone who is deeply religious. No one would ever accuse monastic religious communities of failing to live a balanced life. The motto of the Dominican Order is *Ora et Labora*: Pray and Work, since all religious communities must support themselves even if they are cloistered in a secluded home. In order to be self-supporting, they farm, produce items that can be sold (such as beer and soap), and often work in their local towns and cities. The Daughters of St Paul run bookstores and a publishing house; while the Poor Clares of Perpetual Adoration, run a TV station. In the East, Buddhist monks and nuns continue to work in the monastery and community as laborers and teachers.

A person who is overfeeding their Human Spirit is someone who lives in a way where the *well-being* of their body and mind are completely surrendered to an idealized spirituality. In this "cloud", the Cloud Dweller refuses to tend to themselves or their surroundings. They fail to maintain relationships, and don't earn their keep. Like an over-fed Body, the over-fed Spirit becomes bloated and lazy – a lazy human Spirit begins to turn on itself. Similar to the bloated couch potato body, the bloated human spirit doesn't *do* anything. The Cloud Dweller gazes never-endingly at sunsets without preparing for the next sun*rise*. They don't have the energy to develop their human spirit, while still claiming to be "spiritual". The Cloud Dweller is sitting in place eating the spiritual equivalent of Twinkies and playing the spiritual equivalent of video games, getting spiritually fat. In short: they are stuck in their mother's spiritual basement going nowhere.

What about the person who lives with a malnourished spirit? I call those unfortunates Starving Souls with the same appearance as the person with the overfed spirit. Like the Cloud Dweller, the Starving Soul doesn't engage in life, but for different reasons. They are starving for the Universal Human Goods such as love and beauty, but either lack the capacity or will to obtain it. Without any nourishment for their Spirit, they are unable to generate the emotional energy needed to connect with others or the world around them.

To be clear, I am not referring to a medical or psychological issue that inhibits people from being able to form bonds with others. Instead it is the Starving Soul that keeps the Human Spirit unfulfilled. These poor souls are so malnourished that they are unable to accepted or appreciate the offered Universal Human Goods of love or beauty.

So what does the healthy balanced person who feeds their Human Spirit look like? Their relationships and spiritual practices are *energized,* rather than weighted down. Just as a well-nourished person can enjoy rich fare on occasion, so can a well-nourished Human Spirit be open and accepting to greater, more powerful spiritual experiences.

Those that are spiritually well fed and balanced, are generally happier and will seek out the opportunity to connect with others while engaging in life. The Universal Human Goods of beauty and love are appreciated and are sought within themselves and their surroundings. Their spiritual practices are part of the impetus of their lives, and help them grow. Just like supplying the body good food and exercise to make a healthy body, feeding the Human Spirit with beauty, truth, and love and will make the Human Spirit healthy. Be inspired by something beautiful, cultivate friendships that give you energy, become part of something larger through service or volunteering. These are the things that expand the Human Spirit and keep you growing on the inside as well as out.

courage we might picture something more comical, such as the Cowardly Lion from *The Wizard of Oz*, where we can laugh at the vaudeville humor while rooting for the Lion to *find* his courage.

Physical Courage

Admiral Tarrant from the film *The Bridges at Toko-Ri* asked, "Where do we get such men?" The line is delivered near the end of the film, when the main character fails to return to the aircraft carrier after a mission, and Tarrant looks out at the busy deck and wonders where these men come from and why they serve. That question is a fundamental question people often ask of those who demonstrated courage, and then ask themselves when they look in the mirror. Maybe a better way to ask that question when applied to ourselves is: *Where does courage come from?*

I have given several examples of courage, but it's best to start with my preferred definition of courage

Physical courage is the ability to overcome fear and do what's necessary in order to survive, save a life, accomplish a mission, or excel despite physical or psychological barriers.

Using this definition of physical courage obviously concerns overcoming *external* obstacles. To simplify, demonstrating physical courage is overcoming the "fight or flight" instinct., and choosing to *fight*. Physical courage results in facing danger or the threat of pain to accomplish a goal. Note the danger doesn't have to be *real* – the mere *threat* of danger or pain can be enough to trigger a "fight or flight" response. What is more, "fight" doesn't necessarily mean a physical altercation or use of weapons. In the context of physical courage, "fight" simply involves meeting a particular challenge head on, without avoidance.

> *"Courage is doing what you're afraid to do. There can be no courage without fear."*
>
> *- Eddie Richenbacker*
> *World War I flying ace*

Returning to Admiral Tarrant's question, *"Where do we get such men?"* and rephrasing it to ask *"Where does courage come from?"* There are several answers to that question, it's not as vague as you might think.

There is a physiological reason for courage. Researchers discovered by a very unique (and bizarre) experiment involving snakes and an MRI machine. The Weizmann Institute of Science in Rehovot, Israel, strapped test subjects in an MRI machine with a snake suspended mere inches above their heads. Using the MRI to track brain activity, researchers identified the specific area of the brain associated with courage, the subgenual anterior cingulate cortex (SaCC). Using human's natural snakes to stimulate a fear response, test subjects reported their level of fear as the snake was moved closer and closer until their fear became greater than their courage.[10]

It's an interesting experiment. As researchers are able to determine the role that hormones and pheromones play in the attraction between boys and girls yet cannot define "love", neither can a purely physiological explanation satisfy our curiosity about the source of courage. As I have said many times before, humans are more complex than merely our biology. Surely biology can influence courage – a large person in a crowd of small ones is more apt to be courageous than the opposite. But when it comes to courage, biology is not the determining factor.

History is populated with stories of unexpected heroism from unlikely people. The 98-pound weakling who stands up to the bully on the school yard, and the grandmother who faces down the burglar are legendary, in part because it is documented and has repeated occurrences. Moviemakers have repeatedly made films about the plucky young person who saves the day while facing down a larger and more ferocious enemy. Do these real, and fictional, people have an oversized "courage center" in their brains? Perhaps, but I'd like to think it's more than that.

Can you learn to be courageous? More to the point, can you learn to control fear? Yes, you can. Learning to be courageous has a great deal to do with being prepared. When you have analyzed the "fight or flight" instinct as it relates to the situations you might face, you are much less likely to make a snap decision based on emotion, instead tapping into the wellspring of courage that all people possess. In a way, physical courage is the easiest to understand. We can see the danger being faced, and are able to prepare for it. We can physically prepare, mentally rehearse our response, hone our skills, and work in a team with others. This is applicable to battle scenarios, emergency situations, or even on the sports field. That preparation is key to suppressing the fear response.

When Air Force Academy graduate, former fighter pilot, and USAir Captain Chesley "Sully" Sullenberger landed USAir Flight 1549 in the Hudson, he said in an interview with *60 Minutes* that moments before the crash were "the worst sickening, pit-of-your-stomach, falling-through-the-floor feeling" that he had ever experienced. However, he and his crew had practiced emergency landings with such diligence, that they were able to put that fear aside and skillfully control the emergency landing. His team saved the lives of everyone on board the flight because they didn't succumb to fear. Instead, they controlled their fear.

To paraphrasing a chief master sergeant that I served with during my Air Force career, "Few rise to the occasion in combat. Rather, they sink to the level of their training." The way the military values training, especially the repetition of so-called "perishable skills", is an indicator of the value of preparation. Soldiers expect to face danger, and prepare themselves against fleeing from it. The procedures are rehearsed over and over again until it becomes second nature.

I think courage comes from a well within our Human Spirit. It stems from more than mere biology, since we are more than mere flesh and bone. If humans were only biological machines, would there be an ability to create beauty, love, or be able to discern truth from lies? Biology certainly plays a role in who we are – after all, we are not disembodied spirits – but it cannot offer the entire answer. Courage, like other Universal Human Goods, comes from *both* our biology and our Spirit.

A sense of duty and fraternal love contributes to courage, as does the nearly universal human social need to be accepted among a social group. Soldiers who exhibit courage in combat situations most often report that they were "just doing their jobs" and "didn't want to let their teammates down." We call that "duty" and "loyalty", these qualities are among the most prized of human virtues.

People are willing to endure considerable hardship when they know that others are depending upon them. When that social pressure includes life and death situations, the sense of duty becomes even stronger. Oftentimes, our sense of duty – will override the fear instinct. That is where true courage originates. Ultimately, courage is an act of love. It's the love of others above self that will motivate people to endure hardship and brave danger in order to protect others. Without love, there can be no courage.

The Olympic gymnast is another example, though slightly different. The fear of injury and even death is real, but not from other teams. The gymnast must first conquer himself. In a real way, gymnasts must first conquer *gravity* before they can even approach the "inner voice". Like any sport, being an Olympic level gymnast requires constant dedication and sacrifice. It requires subordination of fear, heights, and pushing pain completely out of the mind to focus on the task at hand. In addition, teammates are depending on a high score. Years of 4 a.m. practices, foregoing social interactions and activities, arriving at the single moment where the difference between a gold medal and no medal is a fraction of a point. If the gymnast makes a mistake in the Olympics, he's not only risking injury, he's letting his country down.

Lastly, consider the courage of the cancer or rehabilitation patient. Both must rise daily with the knowledge they will face pain that day. For the cancer patient, that struggle is an actual fight for their life. Chemotherapy and radiation therapy are *very* hard to endure. There are days of nausea and pain each time. Choosing to fight their disease rather than succumb to it takes a daily dose of special courage. Similarly, the amputee or accident victim who goes to physical therapy knowing they face hours of pain just to *hope* they reacquire skills they once took for granted takes courage. Wounded Warriors in rehab face weeks or even months of painful therapy to learn to walk again, or feed themselves, or hug their lived ones. People who have suffered physical or psychological trauma must daily *choose* not to let their injuries define them, The alternative is to cease to live. That is courageous as well.

Overcoming pressure, the fear of mistakes, and the very real fear of severe injury requires physical courage. To be an

Olympian is to find the courage to succeed even when success is elusive, to manage fear for years in a single-minded purpose to stand on the winner's podium.

Moral Courage

Moral courage is the companion to physical courage. There are hundreds of fictional examples in cinema and literature, as well as real life displays. People that are willing to do the right thing or speak out against social injustice, while understanding that there might be a social or personal cost.

"Moral courage is the most valuable and usually the most absent characteristic in men"

- George S Patton Jr.

There a plenty of examples all around us, people who have steadfastly held to their convictions, those that have chosen to speak up for those that cannot speak for themselves. Mother Teresa of Calcutta actively confronted injustice and challenged the apathetic to act to help alieve the suffering of the people she served. Dr. Martin Luther King peacefully, but determinedly, *required* society to eliminate segregation, and treat all Americans as equals by the sheer force of his words and personal presence. President Andrew Johnson, who succeeded the slain President

Abraham Lincoln, was determined to continue Lincoln's plan to "bind up the Nation's wounds" rather than subject the defeated South to prolonged military occupation and indignity. He suffered public ridicule and eventual impeachment by those in Congress that were motivated by revenge rather than the spirit of conciliation. These, and many others, are examples of heroic moral courage.

John Quinones of the television program *"What Would You Do?"* presents example after example of people "stepping up" to act when their morals or convictions are affronted. It is a comfort to me that *most of the time*, people that find themselves in this type of situation choose to act, rather than let others suffer needless harm. When speaking of people that lack the moral courage to stand up to injustice, Quinones said, *"I think those of us who don't, and don't consider the consequences, have a lot to learn about how to love one another. Let's get involved in the world; let's make this a better place; let's give a damn."*[11]

What *is* moral courage exactly? I have come up with a definition of my own, which is: "The ability to hold firm to one's convictions in the face of criticism or personal attacks."

While only a few of us will ever have to charge into battle, rescue someone from a burning building, or compete in the Olympics, everyone has a daily opportunity to demonstrate moral courage. As the soldier physically and mentally prepares to enter battle, we also have to prepare to be morally courageous when the presented with the opportunity. That sort of daily exercise of the moral courage "muscle" requires both a moral code and an external orientation. The ability to act or make the correct decision in stressful situations, similar to the fortitude required to become a champion athlete, requires repetition and practice. You can't just "start" to have moral courage any more that you can just show up and expect to compete in the Olympics.

How do you train to be morally courageous? First, you have to have a solid moral foundation set in good character – a foundation based on a set of principles that are valued and worth defending. In the same way that it is impossible to stand steady on shifting ground, it's impossible to defend non-existent values. That is the essence of moral courage: being willing to endure criticism and perhaps worse, in order to defend your convictions. Shifting values is called "moral relativism", while allowing the whims and social current to guide you is a road that leads to both sentimentalism and bullying.

> *"We are moving toward a dictatorship of relativism which does not recognize anything as for certain and which has as its highest goal one's own ego and one's own desires."*
>
> *- Pope Benedict XVI*

To be clear, I'm not talking about maturing in your outlook on what's important to you, or even changing your mind. As we grow, we learn new facts, gaining new experiences that change our outlook on life. We learn to apply our principles in new situations, and we certainly encounter much more complex problems as we mature. Each of us has to be able to appreciate the need to deal with things never conceived of in our youth as we mature. This is a skill that is particularly necessary for leaders. However, we will be unable to *consistently* make good moral decisions in unfamiliar circumstances if we don't have a firm set of starting values. The difference between the moral relativist and the principled person is the ability to make those difficult decisions unemotionally, even clinically.

The principled person has two advantages over the moral relativist: they can use logic as well as the virtues of justice and prudence to make decisions, and are able to make those decisions under pressure in new, never-encountered situations. Therefore, the principled person must have, what I call, an "external orientation".

Humans have the remarkable ability of being able to convince themselves of almost anything. It doesn't take much of an internet search to see the extensive range of opinions on mundane topics such as diet and exercise, not to mention important subjects like government policy, religion, or scientific theory. Some of those opinions are informed, others – not so much. The interesting thing about this variety of opinions is the capacity for people to rationalize almost any position. Without a defined set of principles, decisions will be ruled by emotion ("it *feels* right!") or power ("*I'm* the leader, I decide!"). Even unarguable facts will not intrude on the moral relativist's decision making process – as they conflict with the emotion of the moment or the leader's direction. Unless a moral relativist is willing to learn, *facts don't matter*. They will assume that the facts being presented *your facts* and can be dismissed out of hand.

To understand the benefits of being a principled person, consider the analogy of a hike. Navigating from "here to there" along the trail requires the following tools: a map, a compass, and hiking skills. In this example, the map represents life, with marked dangers and trails to navigate. The compass' North Pole represents our principles. The skill at hiking skill equates to the experience and practice gained while making decisions based on those principles.

Anyone that has spent any time in the outdoors knows not every danger is on the map – unexpected events will occur. Furthermore, a trail that looks easy on a well-made map is often confusing on the ground. When I was stationed at the Air Force Academy, I was amazed at the number of people who got lost on the "easy" trails due to taking a wrong turn. Even experienced hikers could find themselves lost on well-travelled trails when they didn't take routine precautions, were over-confident, and made additional bad decisions.

Usually, people would become disastrously lost because they had simply made a wrong turn, then became disoriented and panicked. This situation is comparable to making an emotion-based decision. Emotion clouds our judgment, and prevents us from seeing things clearly (much like simply retracing our steps on the trail to find the starting point). If you have ever been lost and been sure the way back was just ahead, you can appreciate the danger in allowing emotion into your decision-making process. Invariably, decisions made from emotion, rather than principles, are poor decisions that get us even *more* lost, rather than found. When you find yourself experiencing an emotional response to a moral problem, stop and evaluate the situation in light of your principles.

Sometimes the leader is the one responsible. I was on a night hike along with others on a Pacific island. When our beach trail was blocked, we elected to cut across the little island to find another trail – and ended up blundering through the dark jungle and over abandoned World War II trenches. There are any number of things that could have happened from that "boonie stomp" hike – almost all of them bad. Someone could have stepped on an unexploded shell, been bitten by a snake or poisonous insect, or simply turned an ankle by falling into a hole or trench in the dark. Thank goodness we found the trail without any injuries, or worse. But the reason we were "stomping" through the jungle in the first place was because we were following a leader that was *certain* he knew how to get back on the trail. None of us spoke up, even though *all* of us thought it was a horrible idea to get off the beach.

The moral dilemma analogy is a leader directing an action others in the group believe is morally wrong. If you are a principled person, you will have to take a stand if you are being led into a situation that could put you at risk of compromising your principles. To do that, you will need to have rehearsed how to properly use your map and compass.

In addition to being a principled person, you have to practice what you believe *daily*. It does no good to hold onto a set of principles, if you keep them locked in a box and only take them out when you have a major dilemma. If the first time you look at your map and compass is *after* you are already lost, then there is no way that you will be able to determine where you are, let alone chart a course to your proposed destination. This means you need to have your map and compass ready from the beginning and refer to it often. You need to *practice* using your map and compass so that you know how they work and you will be able to understand how to read the map.

Moral courage is like practicing those hiking skills. The daily exercising of the principles used to make moral decisions will make you more capable of making tough decisions as they arise. Is a boss asking you to violate your personal code of ethics? Or perhaps, asking you to violate your morals? Are friends pressuring you to ignore your core values or go against your upbringing? Is a politician appealing to your emotions to gain your vote, despite his political platforms that are contrary to your principles? The only way you will know is if you check your "moral map and compass" to evaluate your position in relation to who you are as a person and where you want to be. To do *that*, you will have to have a working map and compass, have the skills to use them, and the strength and courage to hold to them.

This is how moral courage is developed: by dealing with the small, seemingly insignificant decisions without stress or pressure. Do you perform the inspection, or just sign off on the form? Do you join in with the office gossip, or find a way to turn the conversation to something more productive or informative? Do you leave a note on the windshield of the car you accidentally bumped in the parking lot, or drive away? These are the types of everyday situations that can be used to exercise your "moral courage muscle." Making good decisions repeatedly will prepare you for the really tough decisions in life, where the consequences are far more severe. I know it sounds obvious, but if you truly want to be a person of good character, a morally courageous person – then you must *work on it daily*. Choose your path, align your compass to the North Star of your principles, and stay on the trail.

Summing It Up

No person is perfect, but that lack of perfection should not give us permission to live in mediocrity. *The Five Be's* is a prescription against mediocrity, and provide us with a vision of who we can be, when we are at our best. **Be Proud of Who You Are**, especially when others try to devalue you. **Be Free** of the chains of others' desires or your own appetites: you are so much more than that. **Be Virtuous** and remember that virtues are like the guard rails on the road of life: there to keep you safe rather than hem you in. **Be Balanced** and live a life of significance by developing your whole person, not just a portion of yourself. Finally, **Be Courageous** because to live a balanced and integrated life of virtue in authentic freedom *requires* courage.

You have it in you – unleash the authentic person you know you can be!

Order Form

Email Address: _____
Daytime Phone: _____

Billing Address
Name: _____
Street Address: _____
City / State / Zip: _____
    Country: _____

Shipping Address (if different than Billing Address)
Name: _____
Street Address: _____
City / State / Zip: _____
    Country: _____

Payment Information:
Qty: _____ X $19.95   = _____

Plus Shipping @$2.50/book   = _____
                    TOTAL = _____

Credit Card: MC/Visa Number:
_____
Exp: _____ Security Code: _____

Scan and email to:
Mickey@LeadTheWayMedia.com
www.mickeyaddison.com

Other Books by Mickey

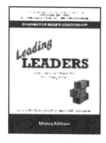

Leading Leaders: Inspiring, Empowering, and Motivating Teams

"Leading Leaders" is straightforward advice for leaders at all levels on how to be successful. Developed over a 26 year military career and a lifetime of leading, Colonel Mickey Addison lays out the foundation for character-based leadership. Illustrated through personal stories and anecdotes, Leading Leaders is a must-read for anyone who wants to improve their productivity and their character.

Leading Leaders: The Workbook

Leading Leaders: The Workbook is a companion to Mickey Addison's acclaimed work by the same title, but can be used as a stand-alone guide for discussion groups, seminars, and individual study. Thoughtful questions and chapter self-assessments will assist leaders and teams to improve their leadership skills through candid review of both leadership and followership skills.

Patio Wisdom: Wise, Inspiring, and Humorous Quips from Living a Life at Full Speed

Welcome to the world of The Patio King! Inside are the musings from Living a Life at Full Speed, where wisdom comes from the School of Hard Knocks. It's wisdom born of adventure and hardship, joy and pain, victory and defeat...and everything in between. Illustrated with the author's own photos, and narrated with quips and memories, Patio Wisdom will leaving you in tears and stitches.

All of Mickey's books are available at his website: www.mickeyaddison.com

About the Author

Mickey Addison is a career military officer, blogger and author of six books, including *Leading Leaders*. He is a frequent contributor to military newspapers and journals, including *Armed Forces Journal*, and *The Military Engineer*. His passion for leadership led him to found his own hobby publishing company: Lead the Way Media to help inspire excellence in business and in life. Mickey is a contributing author at GeneralLeadership.com.

Mickey is passionate about inspiring people to be their best and leading organizations to high levels of performance. As an Air Force officer, Mickey has handled national portfolios totaling billions of dollars. He's presented on dozens of topics to senior leaders in the military, industry, state and federal government, and worked with international business and government executives and in a dozen countries in Asia, Europe, and the Middle East.

Contact Mickey via email at Mickey@leadthewaymedia.com, or through his website: mickeyaddison.com.

End Notes

1. A Japanese term for the man who works in an office, and is wholly dedicated to his company even at the cost of his health and relationships.

2. University of British Columbia. "Pride May Not Come Before A Fall, After All." ScienceDaily. 18 June 2007. <www.sciencedaily.com/releases/2007/06/070615214643.htm>

3. U.S. Department of Health and Human Services. *The Health Consequences of Smoking—50 Years of Progress. A Report of the Surgeon General.* Atlanta, GA: U.S. Department of Health and Human Services, Centers for Disease Control and Prevention, National Center for Chronic Disease Prevention and Health Promotion, Office on Smoking and Health; 2014. <www.surgeongeneral.gov/library/reports/50-years-of-progress/full-report.pdf>

4. National Survey on Drug Use and Health (NSDUH), 2013, National Institute on Drug

Abuse, online, accessed 20 Sep 15, <http://www.drugabuse.gov/publications/dr ugfacts/nationwide-trends>.

5.Alarming Video Game Addiction Statistics, Addictions.com, online, accessed 20 Sep 15, <http://www.addictions.com/video-games/alarming-video-game-addiction-statistics/>.

6. 2008, John Fabry, Allison Miller, Allison Milwid, University of Pittsburgh, online, <http://people.cs.pitt.edu/~mehmud/cs134-2084/projects/Epic_Fail/about.html>

7. Association for Psychological Science. "Childhood self-control linked to enhanced job prospects throughout life." ScienceDaily. 14 April 2015. <www.sciencedaily.com/releases/2015/04/1 50414130403.htm>.

8. Long Workweeks And Strange Hours, Daniel S. Hamermesh and Elena Stancanelli, Working Paper 20449, National Bureau Of Economic Research, Cambridge, MA, September 2014,

<http://www.nber.org/papers/w20449.pdf, 20 Sep 15>.

9. "Physical inactivity a leading cause of disease and disability, warns WHO" World Health Organization Media Center, 4 April 2002, online, accessed 20 Sep 15, <http://www.who.int/mediacentre/news/rele ases/release23/en/>.

10. "Brain's Courage Center Located", Rachael Rettner, LiveScience.com, 23 June 2010, online, accessed 20 Sep 15, <http://m.livescience.com/8342-brain-courage-center-located.html, accessed 20 Sep 15>.

11. "John Quinones, Journalist And Host of What Would You Do? Speaks To University Wednesday Night", The BG News, Bowling Green University, Eric Lagata, Campus Editor, January 29, 2014, online, accessed 20 Sep 15, <http://www.bgnews.com/campus/john-quinones-journalist-and-host-of-what-would-you-do/article_e72e7d00-8962-11e3-95ca-0019bb2963f4.html>